The Centre for Enterprise, Markets and Ethics

Enterprise and Faith Series

God and Enterprise
Towards a theology of the entrepreneur

Edward Carter

Copyright © 2016 by Edward J. Carter
This edition © 2016 by the Centre for Enterprise, Markets and Ethics

The moral rights of the author have been asserted.

All rights reserved. This book or any portion thereof may not be reproduced or used in any manner whatsoever without the written permission of the publisher, except for the use of brief quotations in a book review.

Scripture quotations are from New Revised Standard Version Bible: Anglicized Edition, copyright © 1989, 1995 National Council of the Churches of Christ in the United States of America. Used by permission. All rights reserved.

First edition, 2016
ISBN 978-1-910666-02-9
Published by:
Centre for Enterprise, Markets and Ethics
31 Beaumont Street
Oxford OX1 2NP

Printed in the United Kingdom by Foremost Print Ltd, Unit 9a, Vantage Business Park, Bloxham Road, Banbury, Oxfordshire OX16 9UX
Cover photo by Adam Smok

Contents

1. Introduction — 5
2. The gulf between faith and economics — 9
   - 2.1 Rival promises: God and money — 10
   - 2.2 Rival world views: scarcity and abundance — 17
   - 2.3 Summary — 25
3. The nature of enterprise — 31
   - 3.1 Enterprise and economic theory — 32
   - 3.2 Towards a theology of enterprise — 39
   - 3.3 Summary — 48
4. Closing the gulf: a Christian voice for enterprise in the world — 53
   - 4.1 The Christian entrepreneur in action — 54
   - 4.2 Enterprise as a God-given part of the economy — 59
   - 4.3 The Christian entrepreneur as a 'minister' in the Church — 62
   - 4.4 A personal endnote — 64
   - 4.5 Summary — 65

Chapter 1

Introduction

INTRODUCTION

As a young adult leaving the world of education in the summer of 1988, I was unusual. Many of my peers were going to start careers with large financial companies, and almost all of them had been accepted on to the graduate trainee programmes of publically listed corporations. In contrast, I decided to set up my own business, fired by some deep entrepreneurial instinct within me. I learnt a huge amount very quickly, had some successes, but by 1990 realised that I needed to learn from other entrepreneurs before I could do it myself. I spent the following few years working for two small businesses, each run by their founder, both in their different ways an entrepreneur. Life then took what seemed to be a rather different direction as I responded to the call to full-time ministry in the Church of England. However, finding myself immersed in the study of theology, the lingering question kept reappearing in my mind: could human enterprise properly be described as contributing to God's purposes? Furthermore, could God therefore in some sense be described as an entrepreneur?

On the morning of 8 March 2015, I had been invited to preach at the church of St Mary-at-Latton in Harlow, Essex. In my sermon I used for the first time the expression 'God the entrepreneur'. I attempted to make a connection between two different partnerships: on the one hand, the partnerships that operate on a human level; on the other, the partnership that operates between God and humanity, made real in Jesus Christ. I touched also on the theme of 'attentiveness'. I suggested that entrepreneurs are instinctively attentive people and that they therefore might have a distinctive role in helping to bring together the two great theological themes of creation and fellowship. The response afterwards from the congregation was very striking in its warmth and enthusiasm, and it set me thinking again about enterprise as something at the heart of the Christian gospel.

This publication is aimed at setting out those thoughts in a structured way. My argument has two main preparatory stages, presented in Chapters 2 and 3, followed by a concluding chapter that looks at what a Christian voice for enterprise in the world might be like. Chapter 2 looks at two significant reasons why there might be a gulf between matters of faith and questions of economics: the first is to do with the nature of money; the second is connected with questions of scarcity and abundance. For some theologians this gulf is so wide that there can in practice be little or no engagement with capitalism and market economics. However, my own suggestion, arising out of my experience that Sunday in Harlow, is that enterprise can play an important role in bridging this gulf.

> **'Could God therefore in some sense be described as an entrepreneur?'**

Having suggested such a role for enterprise, Chapter 3 looks at the very nature of enterprise itself. This examination comes in two stages: first, I look at the positive ways the phenomenon of enterprise is incorporated into economic theory and how it can be taken as a key foundation stone of economics; second, I build on these insights to construct the beginnings of a theology of enterprise, using a number of core biblical themes. Having thoroughly examined enterprise from the points of view of both secular economics and of faith, the way is clear to test whether my suggested 'bridging' role for enterprise is in fact sustainable. My argument arrives at the view that enterprise is indeed a remarkably solid bridge, uniquely placed to establish the points of contact between faith and free-market economics.

The concluding chapter takes up this standpoint and applies it in a number of more practical ways. My hope in this is to encourage a Christian voice for enterprise in the world, rooted in theology but realistic about how the world of business and economics actually works. Of course, not everyone is instinctively entrepreneurial, but no one can deny the power of enterprise in shaping society. The argument in this publication aims to shed light on how such a powerful influence should be understood in the light of the Christian faith. My intention is that it should be a help to entrepreneurs as they reflect on their role within society, and that it may also help the Church re-imagine both its place within the world and some of the ways it organises its own patterns of behaviour.

Introduction

At times my discussion becomes quite technical and complex, although my intention is for it always to remain focused on my overall argument. However, it is possible to follow the main thrust of what I am saying by looking at the summaries at the end of each chapter.

Chapter 2

The gulf between faith and economics

Many attempts have been made to apply faith to economics. This is, however, a challenging task to undertake, because of the dislocation between the world as God intends it to be and the world as it actually is. A preliminary step is to accept that faith is real and has something to offer in this sphere. Some would not agree, but for the purposes of this publication I will take this as a given and foundational assumption.[1] Even when this assumption is made, the gulf between faith and economics is significant. Any simplistic attempt to bring the two together will be insufficient, although this has not prevented people from proclaiming idealistic solutions. There are also many examples of serious attempts to bridge this gulf, which look to a variety of ideas right across the political spectrum, from socialism to free-market capitalism.[2] In making a fresh attempt, I wish first to examine in detail two reasons why the gulf exists. My intention is that such an examination will open the way to a re-imagined bridge, one that uses the theme of enterprise in a distinctive way.

2.1 Rival promises: God and money

The first aspect of the gulf between faith and economics is to do with money. This springs out of the biblical injunction that the love of money is a root of all kinds of evil (1 Timothy 6.10). The close examination of the nature of money that follows will show why this is so, but will also reveal a possible point of contact.

2.1.1 The history and nature of money[3]

Room 68 at the British Museum traces the history of money. It begins with exchange tokens, usually metal coins, and then gradually moves on to paper money, starting with a Chinese banknote from 1375. The earliest English banknotes carry messages such as 'The Carlisle City & District Banking Company promise to pay to the bearer on demand at their office here . . .', and then the sum in pounds is written in. Sometimes instead of 'the bearer' a person's name might be inscribed. Such a note is a promise, embedded within human society by virtue of the name of the person or anonymous bearer to whom it has been made, and embedded within the geographical context by virtue of the named location where it can be redeemed for gold.[4]

Such banknotes were 'convertible' when presented at the bank, but the expansion of credit, which did so much to fuel the industrial revolution, came about because banks began to issue many more notes – promises – than they could redeem at any one time. This was profitable because of the ability to earn interest on money lent. The danger lay in the possibility that there would be a run on the bank. The urge to make more profits by over-issuing promises would then end in disaster and collapse of the promise-making institution.

Mainly because of this weakness in the financial system, a further and highly significant step came to be taken. This was the move from 'convertibility' to 'inconvertibility', under which a banknote could no longer be presented at a bank for conversion into something tangible. John Chown narrates this step as follows: 'As one might expect, the normal order of events was for a country first to become familiar with convertible bank notes, and that then, under the pressure of a crisis (usually a war) these should be declared inconvertible.'[5] For example, the UK government suspended convertibility during the Napoleonic wars and then restored it when victory had been achieved. However, by the late 1970s every major currency had become inconvertible. Money had become a system of promises hanging in the air, apparently socially indispensable but never quite redeemable.[6]

2.1.2 THE QUALITY AND FEATURES OF 'MONEY AS A PROMISE'

One of the most powerful things about a promise is that it makes a link between different time periods. A promise made yesterday to visit a distant relative within 24 hours will shape completely the present day, if that promise is honoured. Promises made in the past shape the present. Promises made in the present shape the future. This is true even if they are broken, since patterns of expectation and behaviour are formed around promises, regardless of actual outcomes.

If this is true for promises in general, it is also the case for money in particular. Inconvertible currency, the crowning glory of what Brian Rotman calls 'financial capitalism', is based upon 'a money note which promises nothing but an identical copy of itself'.[7] The security and substance of this apparently precarious promise can only be found in a link to the future. Thus, commenting on the historic change away from convertible banknotes, Rotman observes that what inconvertible currency actually signifies as an item of value in the present 'inserts a radically new time-bound element into what is meant by the term "money"'.[8] In sum, money 'is a sign which creates itself out of the future'.[9] What Rotman means is that the nature of money has become in essence symbolic rather than valuable in itself. The symbol of money points to the future redemption of a promise, without which it has no meaning.

The intrinsically time-bound nature of inconvertible money, as noted by Rotman, sheds light on one particular deeply rooted tension within much economic theory, under which economic 'laws' are presented as being quasi-scientific, universally true and abstracted from any true sense of time. However, the poor predictive powers of such laws seem to indicate that economic theories should in fact be attentive to history, and to the way different time periods and different generations are connected. Economic laws, if such a concept is to be useful at all, need to be properly embedded within the flow of history and time. Recognising money as a promise will help with this aspiration.

Beyond this, 'money as a promise' binds the holder into the society within which the money is circulating. In principle, a tangible possession, such as food or clothing, has value and can be enjoyed alone on the proverbial desert island, just as it can be enjoyed among others in a busy city. This is not so with money. The promise that money represents is meaningless without a society that has created it and accepts it. Money, therefore, belongs as an essential element within an understanding of the nature of politics and society.[10]

Niall Ferguson explains this with reference to what he terms the 'square of power', being the four institutions that he claims are essential as the bases of cohesion and strength in a modern society: a tax-collecting bureaucracy; a representative parliament; a national debt; a central bank.[11] If Ferguson is correct, money as a promise has a central role to play in society, notably through the functioning of the banking system as the guarantor of money promises, and through the operating of the tax system. Randall Wray takes a strong position on this latter point, arguing that money can only be understood with reference to taxes: 'The "promise to pay" that is engraved on UK Pound notes is superfluous and really quite misleading. The notes should actually read "I promise to accept this note in payment of taxes." ... We can conclude that *taxes drive money.*'[12] Wray has reminded us that modern society has the nation state as its framework, and that it is only the state that has the power both to control the money supply and to impose and collect taxes.

Whether or not this is a universal truth, it remains the case that some kind of societal guarantee of the promises

> **'The symbol of money points to the future redemption of a promise, without which it has no meaning.'**

conveyed by money is essential, so that they may be trusted.[13] Society's trust is placed in those who operate the supply of money, being the directors of the central bank and by extension those who direct any other banks that are licensed to operate. Bankers are custodians of promises. Monetary inflation is in essence the devaluing of promises. Hyperinflation is the destruction of promises. In situations such as these the trust placed in bankers is eroded and not easily rebuilt. Members of society are forced to look elsewhere. Mervyn King, the former Governor of the Bank of England, described just such a situation when talking about the Sharia-compliant credit card as part of the BBC Radio 4 series, *A History of the World in 100 Objects*:

When Argentina had its financial collapse and reneged on its national debt in the 1990s, the currency became worthless. And in some of the villages of Argentina the use of IOUs as a substitute for paper currency started to grow up. But, the problem with the IOU is that the U has to trust the I. And that may not always be the case. So what happened was that in the villages some of them would take the IOU to the local priest and ask him to endorse it. And the priest, where he felt that he could judge the character of the person who was owing the money, making the promise, would do so, and the person receiving it would be confident that the person making that promise would certainly not want to renege on a promise that he had made to the local priest. Now here we have an example in terms of the use of religion which was not fundamentally about religion as such, but which was about enhancing the trust that people had in the instrument that was being used.[14]

This account sees the banker replaced by the priest as the custodian of society's promises conveyed by money.[15] God's purposes and promises are implicitly accepted as being more trustworthy than those represented by inconvertible money issued by a bank.

2.1.3 A Christian response to the phenomenon of 'money as a promise'

In the light of the above discussion I wish to argue that a Christian response to money should be a deliberate response to the phenomenon of 'money as a promise', not 'money as a material possession'. This is in direct contrast to one common theological approach to money, which has been to include it with possessions in general[16] and then to encourage a proper, godly use of these material things.[17] Under this approach, personal motivation in how money is used is the most important factor, as well as a stated recognition that all things – including money – actually belong to God, being part of the divine creation, with human beings merely stewards on God's behalf. The model presented is one of good stewardship over money, which in itself is held to be morally neutral.

However, when money is recognised as a promise it can no longer be morally neutral.[18] Simply to say that one must avoid being greedy towards money in the same way that one must avoid material greed in general may not be adequate. Money is a promise, which rivals the promises of God. This explains why, in biblical terms, there is a positive view of the goodness of creation as delighted over by God, while at the same time there are particular warnings against the love of money.

Hebrews 13.5 gives one such warning: 'Keep your lives free from the love of money, and be content with what you have; for [God] has said, "I will never leave you or forsake you.'" This warning is particularly specific in being about money, and explains clearly that the faithful promises of God should stand in place of the promises conveyed by money.

In fact the Letter to the Hebrews is especially rich in using 'promise' language.[19] It can be argued that the interpretative key to Hebrews is the nature and scope of God's promises, how they shape worldly history, and the particular place that Jesus Christ holds within the unfolding and fulfilling of those divine promises. The overall picture is one in which God's promises have an enduring character, securely guaranteed (Hebrews 6.17; 10.23). Within this overarching account the former promises of God are set out: the promise to Abraham that from him many nations would be descended (6.13–15), despite the test that God put him to concerning Isaac (11.17–18); the promise to Abraham, Isaac and Jacob of a place to live (11.9); and the promises made to the faithful people of God through the ages (11.33). Woven into this positive narrative are warnings connected to the apostasy of those who did not accept the covenantal promises of God,[20] and a sense in which, notwithstanding the importance of God's promises, the old covenant is deficient.[21]

The writer is clear, then, that the new covenant in Jesus (8.13) has been enacted through better promises (8.6; 9.15), which those of old were never able to receive (11.39). This is made possible because of the priesthood of Jesus Christ, a theme unique to Hebrews, and it can be suggested that this is because only a priest can act as a secure custodian of God's promises.[22] Looking to the future, believers can inherit these divine promises (6.12), described as the promise of God's rest (4.1), if they show perseverance (10.36).

The final reference to promises in Hebrews comes at 12.26. The ultimate bringing together of heaven and earth is described in terms of a divine promise of 'shaking'. This echoes the language of Matthew 24.29, Mark 13.25 and Luke 21.26, and the phrase 'yet once more' indicates that this truly is a reference to the eschaton (final point of earthly history),[23] both as the culmination of the history of God's promises through *time*, and in terms of the promised renewal of a *place*.[24]

Hebrews 13 then outlines a few of the consequences for Christians, as they live under the shadow of this mighty narrative of divine promises. Verse 5, with its warning about the love of money, makes perfect sense when it is understood as a warning against a set of promises that rival those of God. We have seen how money represents a powerful promise that works through time and in societal locations. We observe in everyday situations the extraordinary and unique grip that money can have over people. We know also, from Hebrews and elsewhere, that God's powerful promises work across time and so as to renew the earth, and we recognise the powerful effects that individuals experience when they accept those divine promises for themselves.

2.1.4 Can the promises of money and the promises of God be reconciled?

The challenge, therefore, for a Christian is to understand how these two 'rival promises' can coexist, and what the relationship between them should be. One common answer is to say that there can be no fruitful relationship. For example, Peter Dominy argues strongly that the 'rival promise' embodied in money must be constrained by force:

> *My own conviction . . . is simply to turn away from the doctrine of free markets that has ruled for too long, and to accept the necessity of much stronger and more extensive regulation of money in all aspects of the economy.*[25]

Another view is seen in Tim Gorringe's response, when he argues for a turn away from capitalist market economics to a system characterised by planning and conservation.[26] Yet another response is to look towards a renewed form of socialism, albeit localised, in which the dangers of the 'rival promise' of money are contained by a shared sense of morality, as argued for by Jon Cruddas and Jonathan Rutherford.[27]

However, accepting that money is a 'rival promise' need not necessarily lead to essentially socialist responses such as these. Richard Higginson, in a review of Dominy's book, says:

A neutral view of money will not suffice; it is a powerful force that threatens to overwhelm us, although more of a temptation for some than others. However, the positive uses of money – an efficient means of exchange, a reward for good work, a spur to responsible behaviour, a means of providing for human needs – do not receive sufficient attention from the author.[28]

> **'At heart this gulf is characterised by the contrast between scarcity and abundance.'**

I believe Higginson's critique has merit, but that it would be strengthened through a consideration of the place for enterprise. Indeed, it is not just that the possibility of enterprise can be added to a list of practical advantages that money opens up. I wish to argue that enterprise is far more foundational in helping us understand the way the 'rival promises' of God and money can be, if not fully reconciled, fruitfully held together. I believe this suggestion is possible mainly because of the close relationship between enterprise and money. Horst Hanusch and Andreas Pyka, in their consideration of the way enterprise is a powerful force that shapes the economy, place particular stress on the crucial role that money and banks play: 'Indeed, the entrepreneur and the banker have to be considered as in a symbiotic relationship: the entrepreneur opens up the possibilities of investment for the banker, and the banker enables venturing possibilities for the entrepreneur.'[29] Arguably, within this symbiotic relationship lies the potential for reconciling the rival promises, at least to some extent. However, before taking up this task I wish to turn to the second main reason why I believe a gulf exists between faith and economics, which is to do with a fundamental difference of world view.

2.2 RIVAL WORLD VIEWS: SCARCITY AND ABUNDANCE

The second aspect of the gulf between faith and economics is connected to the way human beings see and experience themselves in the world. At heart this gulf is characterised by the contrast between scarcity and abundance, a theme that runs right through the Bible and which is exemplified by the account of Jesus at the wedding at Cana in Galilee (John 2.1–11). I will now examine this contrast carefully so as to draw out the significance of the gulf but also to shed light on a potential point of contact, a bridge that can begin to connect the two themes.

2.2.1 THE PARABLE OF THE TALENTS RECONSIDERED

When it comes to the subject of entrepreneurial activity, the parable of the talents (Matthew 25.14–30) is a favourite for preachers and church fundraisers. It is nearly always interpreted as giving encouragement to enterprising forms of wealth accumulation. I wish here to argue that this is in effect a misinterpretation,[30] but that paradoxically the parable reveals some much more secure teaching about the kingdom of God, which establishes one of the foundations for a theology of enterprise.

Almost all commentary on the parable of the talents focuses on the behaviour of the three servants. Thus, for example, Charles Dodd suggests that the parable has as its purpose 'to throw into strong relief the character of the scrupulous servant who will take no risks. It is upon his conduct that the judgment of the hearers of the parable is invited.'[31] This breach of trust is, in Dodd's view, most clearly recognised in pious and legalistic Judaism. The reader is therefore invited, in an exercise of imagination, to take the place of one of the servants, and so to hear and respond to the call to act correctly in this life, indeed quite possibly as an entrepreneur.[32] Under this view it is therefore a parable about moral behaviour. The contrast between the behaviour of the three different servants is taken to illustrate the difference between the teaching of Jesus and that of the Pharisees or other competing traditions.[33] This contrast is then applicable in a more general sense. The effect is to align the parable of the talents with the parable of the sheep and goats, which follows it. The theme of responsible and faithful behaviour, against a backdrop of division and judgement, is stressed.

There are, however, characteristics of this particular parable that do not sit easily with this interpretation. The opening verse clearly implies that the parable is intended to be a description of the nature of the future kingdom of the heavens, with a clear link from 25.14 back to 25.1, which opens the parable of the ten maidens: 'the kingdom of heaven will be like . . .'. This means that the parable should be understood as providing teaching about what it will be like in God's promised kingdom.

This suggestion finds significant and important support in verse 29: 'For to all those who have, more will be given, and they will have an abundance; but from those who have nothing, even what they have will be taken away.' The interpretation of the entire parable hinges upon the perceived relationship between this verse and the rest of the passage. For the dominant reading, with its focus on moral behaviour in this life, to be sustained, verse 29 must be played down, as, for example, by Lane McGaughy, who comments with reference to this verse that 'the parable is also embellished with a hortatory application of early tradition . . . a free-floating logion'.[34] Instead I wish to explore the possibility that verse 29 provides the interpretative key at the heart of the parable, summing up what the kingdom of God will be like.

If verse 29 is taken as the heart of the parable, the entire meaning would be focused on the abundance associated with inclusion in God's kingdom, recognisable also in the 'joy of your master' of verses 21 and 23. This sense of abundance is underlined by the huge sums of money involved, one talent being 6,000 denarii, an amount beyond normal everyday comprehension. Even such vast sums as five or two talents are, however, to be understood as small, as verses 21 and 23 make clear, when compared with the abundance to come. The settling of accounts of verse 19 stands for the measuring of the degree to which individuals mirror in their lives now, and in a limited way, the abundance of God's provision to come. The trading metaphor, so easily taken to stand for effort or human ingenuity, must rather connect to the active recognition, on the part of individuals, of God's generous provision in everyday life, commended by the master in the description, 'you have been trustworthy in a few things' (Matthew 25.21, 23). Faithfulness is giving glory to God for God's abundant provision. It brings with it a sense of trust, and not human striving. Put another way, it places the themes of communion with God and the richness of creation centre stage.

> **'Faithfulness is giving glory to God for his abundant provision.'**

However, the commercial metaphor central to the parable causes some confusion, through the way it seems to commend risk taking.[35] It is important to recognise that the third servant failed on the count of recognising and participating in God's abundant provision (see especially verse 25: 'Here you have what is yours'), not as someone averse to risk, something the parable does not condemn. Comparison with the parable of the sower (Matthew 13.3–9) is instructive. This uses an agricultural rather than a commercial metaphor, but the central point Jesus makes is the same: the kingdom of God is a place where abundance is celebrated by some but not recognised by others. Instead of the illustration of trading for profit, we now have the quality of the soil, but both stand as metaphors for divine blessings and abundant provision. The two parables complement each other well, each emphasising a slightly different aspect of this gospel truth.

Comparison with another 'commercial' parable, that of the labourers in the vineyard (Matthew 20.1–16), reinforces the view that the important matter at hand is not human effort or skill. The message of this parable is that the kingdom of God is characterised by divine generosity, and quite specifically not by human effort or use of talents. The generosity of the householder (20.15) is echoed in the passive verbs of Matthew 25.29, which should be understood as a way of speaking of God without mentioning God by name.[36] At first glance it seems that the parable of the talents and the parable of the labourers in the vineyard contain opposite messages, even though they both use commercial metaphors. One seems to encourage the proper use of talents to work productively, while the other seems to indicate that the amount of toil is not important. But this apparent conflict is resolved when the proper and common meaning is uncovered, being the need to glory and participate in the abundance of God's provision. Both parables unite in witnessing to God's purposes.

It would be quite possible, but I believe wrong, to spiritualise this gift of abundance from God, and to understand it only in terms of love, joyfulness or other spiritual gifts. The advantage of the very tangible commercial setting of the parable of the talents is that it lends support to a tangible understanding of the kingdom of God and so contributes directly to a theology of economics and of enterprise. John Wyclif, in his discussion of this parable, sees it as teaching that righteous people *have* their temporal goods in a higher way than the unrighteous, who simply make bad use of them to their own harm.[37] It can be argued that this insight connects to the awareness that the righteous have of God's gracious and bountiful provision. It is this awareness that means they participate in the economy in a proper way.

Economics is thus reintroduced to the parable of the talents, no longer specifically in terms of a call to maximise commercial return or risk taking but in terms of the God-given context. This overarching context is marked by divine blessings and abundance, within which a true economics under God must take shape. I wish to argue that one often-neglected aspect of the proper human response to these divine blessings is the response of enterprise. However, before considering the actual basis of a faith-informed understanding of enterprise, it is helpful to examine the ways abundance shapes relationships.

2.2.2 HOW ABUNDANCE SHAPES SOCIETY AND HUMAN ACTIONS: A SHORT THOUGHT-EXPERIMENT[38]

Economics is nearly always based on the premise of scarcity and therefore efficient use of scarce resources. However, the parable of the talents points us to a different kind of world view, based on the premise of God-given abundance. A world characterised by abundance might seem unreal, but in fact there are plenty of practical examples of situations in which a tangible abundance exists.

Consider, by way of a thought-experiment, a sandy beach. Although there is a finite amount of sand, for all practical purposes the various people on the beach, all of whom are intent on building sandcastles, face no limit to the availability of their raw material. There is an abundance of sand.

The first thing to notice is that the individuals on the beach do not have to worry about where they will get sand from. They will have to expend effort in digging it up and in shaping it into a castle, but there will not be any need to worry on a basic level about whether the resources are available. This removes any need to control the use of the sand or to ration it. It provides the reality of freedom, not in terms of having a multiplicity of choices but rather in terms of a lack of worry about the consequences of acting. This freedom encourages creativity by removing the necessary caution that scarcity imposes, even if setbacks are still possible.

A second feature of life on the beach is that greed and theft are absent, both having been made meaningless by the context of abundance. This opens up the possibility of a true sense of trust between people – not trust based on contract or legal sanction but trust rooted in the abundant provision of the sand. The focus switches to the creative and entrepreneurial use of the sand itself. The lack of greed on the beach also illustrates the important difference between excess and abundance. Excess is a greedy hoarding of things within a world view of scarcity, while abundance is an alternative world view that abolishes the true meaning of excess and greed.

A third feature is the instinct for generosity. This might seem counterintuitive, since an abundance of sand seems at first sight to preclude the possibility of generous behaviour towards other castle builders. Not only does a gift of sand seem superfluous, since the recipient already has an abundance, but the giver seems not to be giving anything up since she or he will still have an abundant supply. However, I believe the act of giving in a situation of abundance is in reality a purer form of generosity than any other, since it brings no feelings of the need for reciprocation. It is a much more spontaneous and uncalculated thing; the beauty is in the generosity of the gesture rather than the price of the thing. The situation of abundance allows for a true generosity, since the obligations brought on by scarcity are absent. It is interesting to notice that this true sense of generosity does not preclude altogether the possibility of competitiveness. The people involved will still be working on their own sandcastles, and there will be a desire to excel. But it is a competitiveness that somehow enjoys the achievements of others rather than seeing them as a threat.

A fourth feature of the society that is seen on the beach of abundant sand is the practical equality it brings. Everyone can have as much sand as they need. In an important sense, everyone is made tangibly equal by a situation of abundance, even if they do not actually use the same amount of sand. Opportunities are open to all equally, and the need for sand is always satisfied. There is no need to insist that individuals have a legally enforced equality, either through some kind of 'rights' mechanism or through wealth redistribution. Instead it is the abundance of sand on the beach that creates a much more profound equality.

Of course, this thought-experiment seems disconnected from the real economy, in which scarcity is central. My aim is not to try and insist that the real economy should be completely shaped by abundance but to look for points of contact where the types of behaviour seen in the thought-experiment seem to be present in the real economy.

2.2.3 ABUNDANCE AS THE WAY GOD SHAPES HUMAN ACTIONS AND SOCIETY

The thought-experiment on the beach is an abstract idea. However, I want to suggest that all the features outlined within it resonate strongly with the teaching of Jesus about the kingdom of heaven and God's purposes. First, the lack of worry is reflected strongly at Matthew 6.25–33, which is quite clearly connected directly with the abundance found within God's kingdom.

Second, the holding on to of excess possessions is marked as a barrier to the kingdom of God, as is made clear by the gospel episode with the rich young man at Matthew 19.16–22. The teaching that follows this episode demonstrates that it is not by some superhuman power of the will that excess and greed can be overcome, but only through the presence of God. Specifically, it is the abundance of the kingdom, pointed to in the promise of 'a hundredfold' (Matthew 19.29) that precludes greed and excess.

Third, generosity is also a strong biblical theme, within which the generosity of God is to be reflected in human dealings. A true generosity, one not expecting a reciprocal gesture, is encouraged at Matthew 5.38–42.[39] Paradoxically, it is within such a context of generosity that the experience of life becomes one of receiving also (Luke 6.38).

Fourth, equality within the kingdom of God is rooted in the equal access to the grace of God through participation in the body of Christ (see especially Romans 10.12–13; Galatians 3.28; Colossians 3.11; 1 Timothy 2.4). This equal access is foreshadowed in the basic equality that all people have as being made in the image of God (Genesis 1.26), in the equality observed in the distribution of land among the people of God (Numbers 33.54) and in the tangible equality all people will have in the kingdom of God, as demonstrated by the parable of the labourers in the vineyard (Matthew 20.1–15), which is explained by the abundant generosity of God (v. 15).

In sum, the theme of God's abundant provision is strongly biblical and underpins the teaching of Jesus about the kingdom of God and the behaviour of human beings within that kingdom. Put another way, the promises of God are fully honoured and taken up by human beings in what they do. Linking it to my earlier discussion, the rival promise of money is re-imagined and relocated within human relationships. Money is no longer anchored in merely human interactions but in a sense begins to be 'redeemed' by being connected to the promises and purposes of God. This is not achieved through human willpower but through a full and proper appreciation of the world as being shaped by God and God's abundant provision.

> **'Money is no longer anchored in merely human interactions but in a sense begins to be "redeemed" by being connected to the promises and purposes of God.'**

2.2.4 CAN THE RIVAL WORLD VIEWS OF SCARCITY AND ABUNDANCE BE RECONCILED?

God's kingdom and the real economy of today are not identical. Indeed, abundance and scarcity seem to be opposites in the extreme. However, attempts have been made to establish points of contact between the two. One interesting proposal has been made by Albino Barrera, who argues that economic scarcity is a means for human participation in 'God's goodness, righteousness, holiness, providence, and restorative justice'.[40]

However, I believe his approach assumes that neoclassical economics and instrumental rationality[41] are logically prior to the Fall, and depends upon a strikingly positive view of human nature. Put another way, this is not really a reconciliation of two world views, rather a subsuming of one within the other.

A different and well-trodden path has a spiritualising tendency. This asks us to disengage from economics altogether and to subsume the 'mirage' of scarcity within the theological reality of abundance. However, this again is a failure to bridge the gulf, rather an attempt to ignore it.

Instead I wish to propose that the theme of enterprise is uniquely placed to effect a bridge between these two contrasting world views. This is because of the features of entrepreneurial behaviour and its role in the economy. In order to demonstrate why this might be so I will now turn to an examination of enterprise itself, as understood both within economics and theologically.

2.3 SUMMARY

I argue that, for two significant reasons, faith and economics have a gulf between them. First, money can be understood as a promise that rivals the promises of God. This means that the love of money militates against a love of God and that a market economy potentially falls short of God's plan for the world. Second, there is a contrast between a world view of scarcity and a world view of abundance. The reality of scarcity is the foundation on which market economics is based, while the reality of abundance describes God's kingdom. Suggestions for bridging this gulf often fail to take seriously both sides. My thesis is that enterprise is particularly well placed to make a connection between the two.

NOTES TO CHAPTER 2

[1] For one of the classic texts that argues strongly for this foundational assumption, see R. H. Tawney, *Religion and the Rise of Capitalism*, Harmondsworth: Penguin, 1938. Of note also is F. A. Hayek, *The Fatal Conceit: The Errors of Socialism*, London: Routledge, 1988.

[2] For a helpful overview, see M. Brown and P. Ballard, *The Church and Economic Life: A Documentary Study: 1945 to the Present*, Peterborough: Epworth Press, 2006.

[3] For an engaging account of the developments in the importance of money, see N. Ferguson, *The Ascent of Money: A Financial History of the World*, London: Penguin, 2009.

[4] It quickly became a custom for regional banks to add the words 'or in London', a fact that both reflected the prominence of the capital city and added hugely to its financial influence as time went by.

[5] J. F. Chown, *A History of Money: From AD 800*, London: Routledge and the Institute of Economic Affairs, 1994, p. 201.

[6] This is the central thesis of the 'Money Circuit' school of economics, which argues that inconvertible money cannot be seen as a commodity, part of what would in effect be a barter economy, but is a unique phenomenon required as the crucial element in a new kind of economy. See A. Graziani, 'The Theory of the Monetary Circuit', *Thames Papers in Political Economy*, Spring 1989, pp. 1–26.

[7] B. Rotman, *Signifying Nothing: The Semiotics of Zero*, London: MacMillan, 1987, p. 5.

[8] Rotman, *Signifying Nothing*, p. 89.

[9] Rotman, *Signifying Nothing*, p. 96.

[10] Simon Goudsmit comments on this as follows: 'Like money, "the common good", is an abstract concept, with no permanent validity, but nonetheless essential for the arbitrage of values. It is needed as a political instrument to legitimize a trade-off between collective interests or responsibilities with private ones. The common good, like money, is interactive' – S. Goudsmit, *The Limits of Money: Three Perceptions of our Most Comprehensive Value System*, Delft: Eburon, 2004, p. 307. For a collection of essays arguing that choices made over monetary policy are always political and not principally informed

by economic theory, see: J. Kirshner (ed.), *Monetary Orders: Ambiguous Economics, Ubiquitous Politics*, Ithaca, NY: Cornell University Press, 2003.

[11] N. Ferguson, *The Cash Nexus: Money and Power in the Modern World 1700–2000*, London: Allen Lane, 2001, p. 16.

[12] L. R. Wray, *Modern Money Theory: A Primer on Macroeconomics for Sovereign Monetary Systems*, Basingstoke and New York: Palgrave MacMillan, 2012, pp. 49–50.

[13] For a consideration of the way trust operates in different societies, see F. Fukuyama, *Trust: The Social Virtues and the Creation of Prosperity*, London: Penguin, 1996.

[14] BBC Radio 4, 21 October 2010 – see www.bbc.co.uk/programmes/b00vcqcz.

[15] This connects to the idea that all promise-making or swearing of oaths is in some sense sacred: 'Normally when one swears one calls upon God or some other supernatural agent or some sacred person or object or revered institution as part of the mode of achievement of the illocutionary act of swearing' – J. R. Searle and D. Vanderveken, *Foundations of Illocutionary Logic*, Cambridge: Cambridge University Press, 1985, p. 188.

[16] A particularly strong recent example of this bracketing of money with possessions is made by Ben Witherington III: 'It is important from the start to recognize that money is just one sort of asset, one sort of material good that exists in this world, and from a theological point of view all such "stuff" should be discussed together' – B. Witherington, *Jesus and Money*, London: SPCK, 2010, p. 18.

[17] For example, Craig Blomberg concludes: 'A major component of the material dimension is transformation in the way God's people utilize "mammon" – material possessions' – C. L. Blomberg, *Neither Poverty nor Riches: A Biblical Theology of Possessions*, Nottingham: Apollos, 1999, p. 246.

[18] This is the approach taken by, among others, Philip Goodchild and Peter Selby – see P. Goodchild, *Theology of Money*, London: SCM Press, 2007; P. Selby, *An Idol Unmasked: A Faith Perspective on Money*, London: Darton, Longman & Todd, 2014.

[19] Taken together there are 18 examples of the noun 'promise' (*epaggelia*) and verb 'to promise' (*epaggellesthai*), a higher number than in any other New Testament book.

[20] On this point, William Lane observes concerning Hebrews 12.14–29: 'The

writer consistently interprets apostasy with expressions and OT texts that are covenantal in character (3.7–19; 6.4–8; 10.26–31). With the example of Esau, apostasy is defined as a decisive contempt for the gifts of God secured on the basis of covenant and as a rejection of a significant vocation defined through covenant' – W. L. Lane, *Hebrews 9—13*, Word Biblical Commentary, 47B, Dallas, TX: Word Books, 1991, p. 488.

[21] See 7.18–19; 8.7, 13; 9.8–10; 10.1–4, 9.

[22] For an argument that supports this suggestion, see J. M. Scholer, *Proleptic Priests: Priesthood in the Epistle to the Hebrews*, JSNTSup 49, Sheffield: Sheffield Academic Press, 1991.

[23] See: R. P. Gordon, *Hebrews*, Sheffield: Sheffield Academic Press, 2000, p. 160.

[24] On this, Graham Hughes observes: 'It becomes a matter of exegetical judgement as to which of the two schemes – the historical or the spatial – is fundamental to the writer's thought-structures, and which has been introduced in a secondary capacity. But that both are present and that the terms "heaven" and "earth" therefore bear about them an ambivalence requires to be noted' – G. Hughes, *Hebrews and Hermeneutics: The Epistle to the Hebrews as a New Testament Example of Biblical Interpretation*, Cambridge: Cambridge University Press, 1979, p. 45. Better might be to accept that both aspects are equally significant.

[25] P. Dominy, *Decoding Mammon: Money as a Dangerous and Subversive Instrument*, Eugene, OR: Wipf & Stock, 2012, p. 126.

[26] See especially: T. J. Gorringe, *Capital and the Kingdom: Theological Ethics and Economic Order*, London: SPCK, 1994. The final chapter, entitled 'Two Ways', sets out arguments connected to work, the environment, localism, taxes, money, a basic income for all citizens and long-term sustainability (pp. 164–70).

[27] J. Cruddas and J. Rutherford, 'Common Life: Ethics, Class, Community', in A. Pabst (ed.), *The Crisis of Global Capitalism: Pope Benedict XVI's Social Encyclical and the Future of Political Economy*, Cambridge: James Clarke, 2012, pp. 237–54.

[28] Book review, *Theology* 117.3 (2014), p. 219; reviewer's emphasis.

[29] H. Hanusch and A. Pyka, 'Principles of Neo-Schumpeterian Economics', *Cambridge Journal of Economics* 31.2 (2007), pp. 275–89 (pp. 282–3).

[30] Peter Selby argues similarly in his consideration of this parable; see Selby,

An Idol Unmasked, pp. 104–7. However, he is suspicious of a role for human enterprise.

[31] C. H. Dodd, *The Parables of the Kingdom*, rev. edn, Glasgow: Collins, 1961, p. 111.

[32] See, for example, J. M. Ross, 'Talents', *Expository Times* 89.10 (1978), pp. 307–9, which concludes with the connected messages that we must all develop our different capacities, or talents, that church traditions are for use and not just preservation, and that our business in the world is to do good rather than keep ourselves pure. In finding a more explicitly economic meaning within the parable, Manfred Spieker argues: 'The challenge to increase to the best of one's ability the talents placed in one's safekeeping refers to the whole person, and not just one's possessions, but neither are the latter excluded. Property should be used productively and increased' – M. Spieker, 'The Universal Destination of Goods: The Ethics of Property in the Theory of a Christian Society', *Journal of Markets and Morality* 8.2 (2005), pp. 333–54 (pp. 348–9).

[33] Davies and Allison comment that: 'Many now agree that the wicked slave was for Jesus a cipher for his opponents, the scribes and Pharisees' – W. D. Davies and D. Allison, *A Critical and Exegetical Commentary on the Gospel According to Saint Matthew*, ICC, 3 vols, Edinburgh: T. & T. Clark, 1991–7, III, p. 403.

[34] L. C. McGaughy, 'The Fear of Yahweh and the Mission of Judaism: A Postexilic Maxim and its Early Christian Expansion in the Parable of the Talents', *Journal of Biblical Literature* 94.2 (1975), pp. 235–45 (p. 239).

[35] Hence the tendency for commentators to read a need for risks to be taken into the passage; see, for example, D. C. Steinmetz, 'Matthew 25.14–30', *Interpretation* 34 (1980), pp. 172–6 (p. 174).

[36] As suggested by B. M. Newman and P. C. Stine; see *A Translator's Handbook on The Gospel of Matthew*, London, New York and Stuttgart: United Bible Societies, 1988, p. 802.

[37] *On Civil Lordship*, Book 1, chapter 6, as set out in O. O'Donovan and J. L. O'Donovan (eds), *From Irenaeus to Grotius*, Grand Rapids, MI and Cambridge: Eerdmans, 1999, p. 494.

[38] A fuller discussion of this theme can be found at E. J. Carter, 'Abundance, Beauty and Role: Towards a Theological Economics', unpublished MLitt thesis through Oxford University, held at the Bodleian Library, 2006; see

especially pp. 20–31.

[39] This divine dimension to generosity is well captured by David Jasper when he observes that 'a gift, a real gift, is well-nigh impossible' but that 'God was no skinflint. The gift of creation was sheer joy to him, and he was far too good mannered to dictate how the gift was to be used' – D. Jasper, 'Echoes of God's Laughter: Why Theologians Should Read Novels', *Theology* 106.834 (2003), pp. 414–20 (pp. 416–17). For an argument that, in a Christian context, a true gift will reflect the character of God, see R. Williams, 'Making Moral Decisions', in R. Gill (ed.), *The Cambridge Companion to Christian Ethics*, Cambridge: Cambridge University Press, 2001, pp. 3–15 (p. 8).

[40] A. Barrera, *God and the Evil of Scarcity: Moral Foundations of Economic Agency*, Notre Dame, IN: University of Notre Dame Press, 2005, p. 179.

[41] Instrumental rationality assumes that rational behaviour is about using known resources to achieve known aims in an optimal manner. It is a model of means and ends that cannot easily incorporate themes such as 'adventure' or 'regret'. For a full discussion, see S. Darwall (ed.), *Consequentialism*, Oxford: Blackwell, 2003.

Chapter 3

The nature of enterprise

Having hypothesised that an important role for enterprise exists in bridging the gulf between faith and economics, I wish now to examine in some detail what exactly 'enterprise' is, from the points of view both of economic theory and of theology. This will shed light on the very nature of entrepreneurial behaviour and therefore allow my hypothesis to be tested.

3.1 ENTERPRISE AND ECONOMIC THEORY

Enterprise has been integrated into economic theory in a number of ways. However, perhaps the most striking discovery is that for much of the past 70 years there has not been a true place for enterprise within economics.

3.1.1 THE ABSENCE OF ENTERPRISE FROM NEOCLASSICAL ECONOMICS

For many economists working in the post-war era the phenomenon of enterprise has either been a puzzle or an irrelevance. This has been at heart because of their desire to understand economics as a science, involving universal and timeless laws of behaviour. In the natural sciences, chemical elements are known always to react together in a consistent manner regardless of the passing of time or history. In neoclassical economics, the dominant model during the second half of the twentieth century, human beings are seen as analogous to chemical elements, and their economic decision-making and behaviour are deemed to be abstracted from any true sense of the passing of time. Neoclassical economic models are based on the idea of reversion to an equilibrium point rather than a dynamic progression to a new state of affairs.

This has not always been the case among economists. John Maynard Keynes appealed to what he termed the 'animal spirits' and 'spontaneous optimism' within human nature, as the engine for enterprise, within a key element of his general theory. It is worth quoting him at some length:

The Nature of Enterprise

Even apart from the instability due to speculation, there is the instability due to the characteristic of human nature that a large proportion of our positive activities depend on spontaneous optimism rather than on a mathematical expectation, whether moral or hedonistic or economic. Most, probably, of our decisions to do something positive, the full consequences of which will be drawn out over many days to come, can only be taken as a result of animal spirits – of a spontaneous urge to action rather than inaction, and not as the outcome of a weighted average of quantitative benefits multiplied by quantitative probabilities. Enterprise only pretends to itself to be mainly actuated by the statements in its own prospectus, however candid and sincere. Only a little more than an expedition to the South Pole, is it based on an exact calculation of benefits to come. Thus if the animal spirits are dimmed and the spontaneous optimism falters, leaving us to depend on nothing but a mathematical expectation, enterprise will fade and die.[1]

However, in much of neoclassical economic theory Keynes' 'spontaneous optimism' and 'animal spirits' have indeed been dimmed to the point of extinction. This has manifested itself in a variety of ways. First, the need for a theory of entrepreneurship is overlooked because the static model of perfect competition in conventional economics requires the assumption that there is perfect knowledge of the future, which is the same as stating that the future is not a substantive thing. Put another way, in the essentially dynamic world of enterprise the future must be unknown and different from the present, whereas in the normal economic model of perfect competition the future is assumed to look essentially like the present. Second, the standard model ignores the need to examine the means by which the factors of production – land, labour and capital – are combined so as to produce goods and services. Third, there is an assumption that technology is a 'given' or an external factor rather than an integral part of how the economy develops. All three of these assumptions remove the very basis for the existence of entrepreneurs, who fashion their role out of an ability to foresee future developments in the economy more

> **'For many economists working in the post-war era the phenomenon of enterprise has either been a puzzle or an irrelevance.'**

accurately than others, and who have the skills needed to recognise valuable technological developments and to bring the factors of production together successfully in innovative ways. Enterprise is therefore in effect ignored, and 'scientific' timelessness retained within neoclassical economics.[2]

Part of the problem here is that money has been incorrectly described by neoclassical economics. As I argued earlier, money properly understood is a promise. It connects people together in a way that a promise always does, and it connects the present with the future. However, conventional neoclassical economics understands money as being nothing more than an effective instrument of barter, one commodity among all others. The distinctive characteristic of money under this view is that it is a convenient medium of exchange, easily divisible and transportable. The important time-connected aspect of money is overlooked. Again, this has not always been the case within economic theory, and there is now a growing sense that money and the banking sector need to be understood in a distinctive manner, not just as a market sector that is essentially the same as all others.[3] Only once the true nature of money is recognised does the stage open up for entrepreneurs to operate on. This is because enterprise shapes the future in dynamic ways, just as a promise does.

> **'Money properly understood is a promise.'**

3.1.2 THE PRESENCE OF ENTERPRISE WITHIN ECONOMIC THEORY

As was seen above in the work of Keynes, enterprise did once have a significant place within theoretical economics, and notwithstanding the above discussion this has been reflected in various ways.[4] Perhaps the most significant economist in this regard is Joseph Schumpeter. He is a rarity as an economist because of his practical experience as a finance minister of Austria in 1919, and his business career, which included some successes but also saw him declared bankrupt in 1924. Eventually he became a professor at Harvard University. Some aspects of Schumpeter's work are challenging, notably his belief that capitalism would eventually collapse under the weight of its own contradictions and be replaced by some kind of socialism. Most commentators now believe he was simply wrong about this, although some are still waiting. However, Schumpeter's theories place enterprise centre stage, and offer a realistic model for money and the banking sector.[5]

At the heart of Schumpeter's approach is the claim that 'the subject matter of economics is essentially a unique process in historic time.'[6] His well-known theory of 'the process of creative destruction'[7] is the principal means by which he imports a sense of dynamic movement and real history into economics. As he states, 'capitalist reality is first and last a process of change',[8] and any point of static equilibrium within an economy must be understood as being a tiny subset within a bigger picture, a subset that, in practical terms, is either rare or non-existent.

Schumpeter thus turns economic theory on its head. The usual neoclassical view that the economy is essentially in equilibrium, or moving towards equilibrium, is replaced with the proposal that the economy is plotting a path through time and is 'a history of revolutions'.[9] It is the new inventions and new developments, being the dominant features on the landscape of economic history, that form the concrete revolutionary steps, and examples, in any industry, are easily to hand. Without these advances the economy is static, merely refining and adding to existing productive methods. As Schumpeter observes, 'add successively as many mail coaches as you please, you will never get a railway thereby.'[10]

It is easy to see, therefore, why Schumpeter, eschewing the static model of the economy, needs a proper theory of enterprise and of entrepreneurs and their motivations.[11] For him, the heart of economic development lies in the genuine newness and discontinuity of whatever it is that is brought about by the entrepreneur, and not in shifting patterns of demand on the part of customers:

These spontaneous and discontinuous changes in the channel of the circular flow and these disturbances of the centre of equilibrium appear in the sphere of industrial and commercial life, not in the sphere of the wants of the consumers of final products.[12]

This is significant because it moves the prime motivational spark within economic theory away from a hedonistic, or even utilitarian, starting point and replaces it with a different kind of motive power. Because the utilitarian model is essentially static, lacking any true sense of time and history, Schumpeter points to the fact that under the instrumental form of rationality associated with utilitarianism, the entrepreneur is in fact irrational:

> *Experience teaches, however, that typical entrepreneurs retire from the arena only when and because their strength is spent and they feel no longer equal to their task. This does not seem to verify the picture of the economic man, balancing probable results against disutility of effort and reaching in due course a point of equilibrium beyond which he is not willing to go. Effort, in our case, does not seem to weigh at all in the sense of being felt as a reason to stop. And activity of the entrepreneurial type is obviously an obstacle to hedonist enjoyment of those kinds of commodity which are usually acquired by incomes beyond a certain size, because their 'consumption' presupposes leisure. Hedonistically, therefore, the conduct which we usually observe in individuals of our type would be irrational.*[13]

This emphasis on personal weight of character on the part of entrepreneurs, and on their possession of 'super-normal qualities of intellect and will',[14] resulting in a high level of initiative, leads Schumpeter to suggest an alternative model of rationality, which he terms 'energetic egoism'.[15] This is to be understood as presupposing 'aptitudes differing *in kind* and not only in degree from those of mere rational economic behavior'.[16] The motivations underlying this energetic rationality Schumpeter identifies and organises under three distinct headings. The first is 'the dream and the will to found a private kingdom, usually, though not necessarily, also a dynasty'.[17] The second is 'the will to conquer: the impulse to fight, to prove oneself superior to others, to succeed for the sake, not of the fruits of success, but of success itself'.[18] The third is 'the joy of creating, of getting things done, or simply of exercising one's energy and ingenuity'.[19]

The temptation is to conceive of Schumpeter's energetic rationality in strongly personal terms, as a description of individual creativity and expression.[20] This would be a mistake, since his argument is cast in terms of social structures and of the entrepreneurial class. This is underpinned when it comes to his detailed description of the entrepreneurial function, a function that 'does not essentially consist in either inventing anything or otherwise creating the conditions which the enterprise exploits. It consists in getting things done.'[21] Here Schumpeter identifies the difference between inventiveness and enterprise. The former is something personal, detached, as it were, from society, while the latter must be understood as being primarily a function that can only be described within the context of society.

An important conclusion that can be drawn out of this distinction is one that sheds light on the source or locus of the entrepreneurial spirit. Neoclassical economists have a fondness for so-called 'external factors', being those given and unchanging – at least in the short term – aspects of the economy. It would be easy to argue that enterprise is just one of those factors, contained within the cultural landscape. However, Schumpeter's analysis would seem to be more adventurous, placing the entrepreneurial function within the fluctuations of the structures of society, and seeing it as being connected closely with the process of effecting new things in a social context rather than in the abstract. Enterprise thus represents, in Schumpeter's analysis, the key example of an activity that connects in a dynamic manner the unfolding of history to the structures of society.[22]

However, a further very important conclusion arising out of Schumpeter's description of enterprise connects back to the individual entrepreneur. The distinction between an inventor and an entrepreneur is seen in the *attentiveness* the latter has to the world, and it is this theme of attentiveness that has been prominent in other considerations of enterprise. One distinctive contribution has been made by Israel Kirzner.[23] He places particular stress on the way the entrepreneur seems to bring new things about by imagining the possibilities that lie ahead. As Kirzner observes: 'We call this motivated propensity of man to formulate an image of the future man's *alertness*.'[24] For Kirzner, this innate human attribute constitutes the heart of enterprise:

It will surely be acknowledged that this alertness – which provides the only pressure to constrain man's envisaged future toward some correspondence with the future to be realized – is what we are searching for under the phrase 'the entrepreneurial element in human action.[25]

The qualities linked to this alertness include 'vision, boldness, determination and creativity'.[26]

Kirzner's approach is echoed in the popular and influential book *Where Good Ideas Come From*, by Steven Johnson.[27] His discussion includes themes such as 'the adjacent possible', 'liquid networks', 'the slow hunch' and 'serendipity'. One section illustrates the importance of the humble commonplace book in the history of innovation and new ideas.[28] What Johnson describes is akin to Kirzner's alertness – a practical means by which closer attention is paid to the world and new possibilities imagined.

3.1.3 CONCLUSION: THE CORE FEATURES OF ENTERPRISE IN ECONOMIC THEORY

We are now in a position to sum up the core features of enterprise as, I believe, best explained by economic theory. Although in some models it is a rather mysterious external factor, the arguments of Schumpeter and others suggest persuasively that enterprise should be at the heart of economics, understood as the key descriptor of the relationships that give shape to the economy. These relationships are manifested in two connected ways. The first is on a macroeconomic level, as described in Schumpeter's social and historical world view. It is enterprise that shapes the big changes and movements in the economy, and therefore contributes powerfully to the unfolding of history and to the structures of society. The second is on a microeconomic level, as captured by Kirzner's theme of alertness. This describes an individual's relationship with the world around her or him, and provides the basis for an imaginative engagement with it.

> **'Enterprise, in fact, should be understood as a central feature of all relationships.'**

I believe it is this 'relational' aspect of enterprise, both on the level of society as a whole and on the level of individual relationships, that is its core and distinctive feature. Under this view, enterprise is not *initially* about innovation or creativity. Instead it springs first of all from the relationships embedded in any human community. Enterprise, in fact, should be understood as a central feature of all relationships, although of course like any feature it can be present or absent in varying degrees. As Roger Koppl observes: 'Entrepreneurship is an aspect of all human action. Entrepreneurship is a human universal. If so, then entrepreneurship theory must be a part of a broader social theory that encompasses many areas, including sociology, psychology, economics, and finance.'[29] My intention now is to demonstrate how theology can be added to Koppl's list.

3.2 TOWARDS A THEOLOGY OF ENTERPRISE

I wish now to introduce one main and two subsidiary theological themes, which will be applied to the phenomenon of enterprise. My aim is to sketch out a robustly Christian and positive understanding of entrepreneurial human behaviour.

3.2.1 THE 'ENTERPRISE' OF THE RESURRECTION PROMISE

Enterprise is often connected to creativity and then theologically to creation.[30] However, I believe the theme of resurrection, or 'new creation', is richer. Resurrection and creation are closely linked in any case, but resurrection is not simply a restoration of something original and pristine. This is evident from the wounds in the resurrected Jesus, which reflect something of the glory of God's purposes. The wounds of Jesus are not removed as he is 'made new' in his risen life. This is a new creation that only makes sense with reference to what has gone before. In other words, resurrection is creation linked theologically to history.

> **'Enterprise is often connected to creativity and then theologically to creation.'**

This observation resonates closely with Schumpeter's view of enterprise, which he argues is the key factor that shapes economic history. We need now to place that powerful insight alongside the theological truth that the resurrection of Jesus Christ definitively shapes history and makes sense of it. While these two 'world views' might be in conflict or rivalry, an alternative possibility is that they are mutually involved, or even mutually implied, and that a world view based on the hope of the resurrection shares points of contact with a world view that affirms entrepreneurial human behaviour.

One particular way the 'resurrection world view' has always been embraced by Christians is in the Lord's Supper, also known as Holy Communion or the Eucharist, which takes its meaning from the death and resurrection of Jesus. Chapter 6 of John's Gospel, while not giving an account of the Last Supper itself, provides the basis for an understanding of Jesus as the bread of life. This chapter is striking in the way it takes up the exodus tradition of the manna in the wilderness as a foundation for explaining the distinctive newness of what God has done in Jesus Christ. Exodus 16 describes God's provision for the people in the form of manna. It is a description that echoes powerfully the thought-experiment of the sandy beach. In short, it is an account of the way the abundance that comes from God shapes human actions and history. Both in John 6 and 1 Corinthians 10 this account is taken up with reference to the Lord's Supper and to the death and resurrection of Jesus. Therefore it can be seen that the core Christian model for human life together is anchored in Jesus, the bread of life, which in turn is understood and explained with reference to the abundant provision made by God in the manna. The resurrection promise in Jesus Christ is grounded in the abundance of a God-shaped world.

My claim now – and this forms a centrepiece of my entire argument – is that *all of these practical aspects of this 'resurrection promise' world view resonate strongly with an entrepreneur's way of seeing the world and acting within it.* Put another way, the kind of world entrepreneurs seem implicitly to recognise around them feels rather like an understanding of the world that accepts the truth of the resurrection of Jesus Christ and the promise of 'new creation' – a world in which the reality of abundance from God shapes behaviour and life. This is a bold and perhaps challenging claim, but I believe it can be supported securely in the following six ways.

1. Entrepreneurs resist any tendency towards top-down social control or rationing. An enterprise economy stands in stark contrast to a planned or 'command' economy. In theological terms, the 'control' is expressed in the

putting to death of Jesus, a moment when a human plan came to fulfilment. However, the abundance of God's provision overcame even this seemingly irreversible plan. The resurrection of Jesus is recognised as the moment when the 'control' represented by the death penalty of the cross is set aside. Life is no longer 'rationed'. On the beach of abundant sand there is no place for rationing or control. This is the world in which entrepreneurs instinctively operate.

2. Entrepreneurs are notably prone to extraordinary efforts and hard work, while seemingly not brought to a halt by anxiety even when a particular attempt at enterprise fails, sometimes several times. Jesus combined both of these aspects of life in his teaching about the kingdom of heaven, which describes life in a world shaped by the resurrection promise. This is carried through in the account of the risen Jesus with the disciples recorded at John 21.1–14. The task of work on a fishing boat, which initially met with failure, is combined with the subsequent presence of the risen Jesus and the overcoming of anxiety through the reality of abundance, reflected in the great catch of fish.

3. Entrepreneurs thrive on the freedom to be creative, this being their main motivation, and not a greedy desire for excess wealth or to do others down. This, at least, was Joseph Schumpeter's central argument, and it is widely reflected in reality.[31] It might be possible to interpret the resurrection of Jesus as a selfish or 'greedy' thing, which was principally for his own benefit, but this would be wrong. A theological understanding of the resurrection of Jesus connects it fundamentally to the powerful gift of freedom and life for others. This is the theological heart of Paul's letters, as exemplified by 1 Corinthians 15.

4. Entrepreneurs are notably trusting and willing to take risks, sometimes to an extent that seems to offend against prudent caution. In fact prudence and caution are not leading characteristics displayed by entrepreneurs. Rather, these characteristics are associated with professions in which the balancing of risks and the safeguarding of positions is more important that the risk of trusting others. It is important to distinguish between risk and recklessness. Risk is associated with trust and therefore with an attentive imagination.

Recklessness is a failure of imagination. At heart, the resurrection of Jesus is about the imaginative possibilities of the new creation, in which God's abundant provision is recognised.

5. Entrepreneurs are always competitive but also generous. This paradox was explained in the illustration of the sandy beach, where it is the abundance of the sand that allows both forms of behaviour to coexist and make perfect sense together. Generosity in theological terms is based on grace, which is manifested in the free gifts offered by God to creation. These are underpinned by the free gift of resurrection, which is guaranteed in turn by the resurrection of Jesus Christ. None of this, however, precludes the kind of striving for fullness of life that Paul describes in his letters and which is akin to the competitive striving of an entrepreneur.

6. Entrepreneurs have a deep appreciation of equality, since they are not constrained by inherited inequalities, instead remaining focused on future possibilities. In historical terms it is entrepreneurial activity that changes the distribution of wealth. Inequitable feudal structures were no longer left untouched but challenged and often overturned. Without enterprise the structures of society are either preserved through the generations or are moulded by the exercise of direct political power. In theological terms, resurrection is a bringer of equality in that it is freely offered to all by God and removes the hierarchies based on inheritance and inherited social structures, since these depend on the reality of death.[32]

> **'A "resurrection world view" resonates strongly within a world shaped by human enterprise.'**

Each of these six short paragraphs sets out in embryonic form a theological point of contact between enterprise and resurrection. Of course, not every entrepreneur in the real world exhibits all of these characteristics, and enterprise is never a direct replacement for resurrection. However, I have argued the deeper point, that a 'resurrection world view' resonates strongly within a world shaped by human enterprise. More than this, no other organising principle for society or human motivation can stand up as effectively when measured against the abundance of God's provision as seen in the manna of Exodus 16, in the Lord's Supper and in the resurrection hope. In sum, I believe the 'resurrection promise' world view, properly understood, provides a rich basis for a fruitful theological appreciation of enterprise and human entrepreneurs. What is more, it can be strengthened in two further significant ways, as follows.

3.2.2 The 'enterprise' of the Holy Spirit

The sermon in which I first used the expression 'God the entrepreneur' (see introduction above) was not based on the parable of the talents. Instead my text was Philippians 3.10: 'I want to know Christ and the power of his resurrection and the sharing of his sufferings by becoming like him in his death.' These words describe Paul's desire to participate fully in everything God has offered him in Jesus Christ. In the original Greek the word translated here as 'sharing' is *koinonia*. Usually this is taken in rather a static sense, and often it is translated 'fellowship'. But I believe a better interpretation is to understand what Paul describes in much more dynamic terms.

The precise word *koinonia* is used three times in Paul's Letter to the Philippians. The first occurrence is at 1.5, where the Philippians themselves are described as partners in the work of proclaiming the gospel. Second, Philippians 2.1 describes a partnership with the Holy Spirit. Finally, Philippians 3.10, as set out above, points to a partnership with Christ, both in his death and his resurrection. Taken together these three occurrences paint a picture of Christians being in tune with the purposes of God, not in a rather static 'sharing' of something but in what might even be described as an entrepreneurial partnership.[33] As Gordon Fee observes of *koinonia*: 'Although this word is usually translated into English as "fellowship," its primary referent is to *participating in* something, rather than to sharing something in common with others.'[34]

Paul's Second Letter to the Corinthians includes examples of *koinonia* that refer to marriage (6.14), to the financial collection being made for the Christians in Jerusalem (8.4 and 9.13) and to the participation of life in the Holy Spirit that believers enjoy (13.13) – part of a short prayer often called 'the grace' that has come to be used very widely among Christians. These different examples are mutually informative. Human relationships, including those of an entrepreneurial nature, are to be understood with reference to the way human beings participate with God in their lives. In particular, the two examples of *koinonia* found in 2 Corinthians at 8.4 and 9.13, which are connected to the Jerusalem collection, are part of an important section of teaching about generosity. As part of his explanation Paul refers back to Exodus 16 when he cites from the Hebrew Bible: 'The one who had much did not have too much, and the one who had little did not have too little' (2 Corinthians 8.15, based on Exodus 16.18). Once again a theological link between the abundance of God's provision and enterprise has been revealed, this time in the 'enterprise' of the Holy Spirit.

The key verse is 2 Corinthians 9.12, which I suggest is best understood as the culmination of Paul's argument. In this verse the practical living out of *koinonia*, according to Paul, results in two things. The second consequence is an overflowing of thanksgivings to God, being the honour and glory due to God in response to his generosity towards creation. However, the first consequence is that the needs of the saints are supplied. The Greek word normally translated as 'supplied' is *prosanaplerousa*, a verb that occurs in the New Testament only here and at 2 Corinthians 11.9, where Paul describes how his Macedonian friends supplied his needs when he was in Corinth, that he might not be a burden to the Corinthians. Although this can be interpreted as a redistribution of defined resources, it is possible to suggest that Paul has something more entrepreneurial in mind.

Within the same overall argument, at 2 Corinthians 9.10 Paul writes of God supplying God's bounty in creation, but the verb used here is *epichoregeō*, in contrast to 9.12. This other verb is also used by Paul to describe the way God directly supplies needs at Galatians 3.5 and Colossians 2.19. However, the use of *prosanaplerousa* at 9.12 hints that something extra or slightly different is going on. In Acts 18.3 we are told that Paul when in Corinth was engaged in his trade of tent-making, and my suggestion is that in this letter he is explicitly picking up on his own example of personal enterprise, within the context of God's abundant provision, to sketch out a vision for human *koinonia* that embraces entrepreneurial behaviour.

My argument has drawn in rather a complex way on the detail of Paul's use of certain words. However, in sum I have suggested that Paul is describing two closely linked things. The first is God's generous and abundant provision and the second is the way human beings can mirror this through the 'enterprise' of the Holy Spirit. Paul does retain the distinction but he also embraces surprisingly warmly the connection between the two as he describes the creative ways human enterprise can contribute to the purposes of God. I believe his arguments form a significant element within a robust theology of enterprise.

3.2.3 THE 'ENTERPRISE' OF PROPHECY

Prophecy is not fortune telling. Rather, a theological understanding of prophecy is that the prophet sees things as they really are, and ultimately sees things as God sees them and as God always intended everyone to see them, which is to say a world marked by abundant divine provision.[35] Walter Brueggemann has expanded upon this core concept of true prophecy by using the theme of imagination and by suggesting that prophets imaginatively see things in a way other people do not. Thus according to Brueggemann, prophets, 'in extraordinary acts of courage, spoke about possible futures that invited Israel beyond its several fissures, when dominant Israel had arrived at despair'.[36] A similar picture is painted by John Goldingay when he states that the prophetic ministry is exercised 'by showing an extraordinary awareness of facts, insights or truths about the past, the present or the future'.[37]

Beyond this, Brueggemann builds on the themes of attentive awareness and insight to suggest that the prophet can access sources of divine energy by using the language of amazement, which is 'the ultimate energizer in Israel, and the prophets of God are called to practice that most energizing language'.[38] It is important to note that this divine energy does not come through the monarchy in Israel, or any other apparatus of the state. Instead it is the prophets, often viewed as troublemakers by their contemporaries, who see things in the correct way and are therefore able to release the energy needed for the common good. Put another way, it is the difference between an entrepreneurial imagination and a top-down strategic plan.

The way prophecy is based on true sight and attentiveness has, I believe, a significant point of contact with Kirzner's theme of alertness, considered above, and which he saw as providing the basis for the way entrepreneurs engage imaginatively with the world. Just as a prophet must be acutely attentive to what is happening in the world, so too an entrepreneur first and foremost must be alert and attentive to what is happening in her or his particular community, tuned in to people's aspirations and frustrations, looking always for opportunities to catch their imagination. The difference, perhaps, is that the prophet is Spirit-filled, attentive to the purposes of God and to the resurrection world view set out above. However, there is nothing to say that an entrepreneur cannot share some of this, and even if this aspect may sometimes be weak, it remains the case that the principles underlying both prophecy and enterprise are strikingly similar. It is as if the features of entrepreneurial behaviour are shaped so as to have the ready potential of contributing positively to God's purposes.

My argument here is based on the observed correspondence between prophetic and entrepreneurial patterns of behaviour. Human enterprise is thereby recognised as having all the potential to be put to work in God's service because of the attentiveness it requires and because of the extraordinary energy it releases.

3.2.4 A THEOLOGY OF ENTERPRISE

In conclusion we can see that the principal theological theme – the 'enterprise' of the resurrection promise – is supported and strengthened by the two subsidiary themes of the 'enterprise' of the Holy Spirit and the 'enterprise' of prophecy. The three themes are tightly linked together. Prophecy is closely connected to the work of the Holy Spirit. In biblical terms this is made quite clear in the Old Testament[39] but comes to fruition in the life of the early Church. There are various accounts in the book of Acts of the Holy Spirit's presence in the words of early Christians who are specifically described as prophets.[40] However, the most significant explanation of this link is found in 1 Corinthians 12. There Paul considers the spiritual gifts (v. 1), being the human vocations empowered by the Holy Spirit for the common good (v. 7). Prominent among this list is the gift of prophecy (vv. 10, 28; see also 14.1).

What is more, there is a sense in which Jesus of Nazareth himself exercised a prophetic ministry, teaching about the good news of the kingdom of God and speaking always of God's purposes. However, Jesus is more than a prophetic voice. He also embodies the very basis by which God's purposes are realised. He contains within his actual being the resurrection promise, which shapes all time and every place. Thus Jesus transfigures and fulfils prophecy. This is seen powerfully in the prophetic words spoken by Zechariah at the moment when his son John was named (Luke 1.67–79). The prophecy is spoken in the power of the Holy Spirit (v. 67) and in continuation of the true prophecy from God, which had come before (v. 70). It is a prophecy that focuses on Jesus (v. 69), points to the ancient promises of God (vv. 72–73) and looks to the resurrection promise (v. 79) that brings salvation in Christ (vv. 69, 77).

This culminates especially clearly in the first recorded public words of the adult Jesus in Luke's Gospel, when he read, as an act of fulfilment, from the scroll of the prophet Isaiah:

The Spirit of the Lord is upon me, because he has anointed me to bring good news to the poor. He has sent me to proclaim release to the captives and recovery of sight to the blind, to let the oppressed go free, to proclaim the year of the Lord's favour. (Luke 4.18–19; based on Isaiah 61.1–2a; 58.6)

It might seem bold to interpret this moment when Jesus sets out his manifesto as summing up the basis for a theology of enterprise, but in a very practical way I believe this is possible. The aspiration that lies at the heart of enterprise is that good news will indeed be brought to the poor as they are invited to participate in the abundant provision that comes from God and are encouraged to imagine a re-energised future. The freedom and release Jesus proclaims is in tune with the kind of creative freedom enterprise springs from. Of course, enterprise is not to be mistaken for the means by which the final fulfilment of prophecy is brought about. It is, however, a very significant aspect of the shape of the world as properly understood within God's purposes.

The rival promises of God and money still persist. The rival world views of scarcity and abundance continue. The role of enterprise within this world of opposing claims on human attention is to provide a creative way – I would argue *the most* creative way – that the promises of God can flourish from within the busy-ness and business of human society and marketplaces.

3.3 SUMMARY

I argue that enterprise is needed as a central element within economic theory, following the insights of Joseph Schumpeter. This is fundamentally because the future is different from the present and because economics cannot solely be about reversion to an equilibrium point. This has the effect of locating economic theory within the flow of history, rather than assuming it to be quasi-scientific and abstracted from time. I also draw attention to Israel Kirzner's argument that the essence of entrepreneurial behaviour is 'alertness' or attentiveness towards society and the world. I then introduce three biblical themes: resurrection, Holy Spirit and prophecy. I demonstrate how these themes connect with enterprise and come together to form the basis for a theology of enterprise. My suggestion is that human enterprise is therefore conceptually especially able to bridge the gulf I previously identified.

Notes to Chapter 3

[1] J. M. Keynes, *The General Theory of Employment, Interest and Money*, London: Macmillan, 1936, pp. 161–2.

[2] Harold Lydall comments on this as follows: 'Entrepreneurship is a subject that is never integrated into the body of neo-classical theory, since it is, of course, logically impossible to do so' – H. Lydall, *The Entrepreneurial Factor in Economic Growth*, London: Macmillan, 1992, p. 58.

[3] For a presentation of the 'historical' approach to money taken by Sir John Hicks, see G. Fontana, 'Hicks on Monetary Theory and History: Money as Endogenous Money', *Cambridge Journal of Economics* 28.1 (2004), pp. 73–88. Fontana concludes: 'Money is the flow of the means of payment used for the production and the circulation of commodities. Money is the stock of liquidity held to meet unforeseen and unforeseeable payments. The supreme challenge for economists is to introduce money in its entire complexity on the very ground floor of economic analysis; to abandon the idea of representing modern economics by timeless barter economy models' (p. 85).

[4] For a fine review of this field, see S. C. Parker, *The Economics of Entrepreneurship*, Cambridge: Cambridge University Press, 2009; chapter 2 is entitled 'Theories of Entrepreneurship' (pp. 31–85). See also Peter Sedgwick, 'Enterprise', in P. B. Clarke and A. Linzey (eds), *Dictionary of Ethics, Theology and Society*, Abingdon: Routledge, 1995, pp. 287–9, which sketches out the history of the theory of enterprise within economics, with its roots in France.

[5] See especially the chapters entitled 'Value and Money' and 'Money, Credit, and Cycles' in J. A. Schumpeter, *History of Economic Analysis*, New York: Oxford University Press, 1954.

[6] Schumpeter, *History of Economic Analysis*, p. 12.

[7] This is the heading of chapter 7 in J. A. Schumpeter, *Capitalism, Socialism and Democracy*, 5th edn, London: Routledge, 1992 (pp. 81–6).

[8] Schumpeter, *Capitalism, Socialism and Democracy*, p. 77 (note 5).

[9] Schumpeter, *Capitalism, Socialism and Democracy*, p. 83.

[10] J. A. Schumpeter, *The Theory of Economic Development: An Inquiry into Profits, Capital, Credit, Interest, and the Business Cycle*, trans. R. Opie,

Cambridge, MA: Harvard University Press, 1936, p. 64 (note 1). First published in German in 1911.

[11] He makes the point, stated in reverse, as follows: 'in a stationary economy, even if disturbed by action of external factors, both the entrepreneurial function and the entrepreneurial profit would be absent' – J. A. Schumpeter, *Business Cycles: A Theoretical, Historical, and Statistical Analysis of the Capitalist Process*, 2 vols, New York: McGraw-Hill, 1939, p. 105.

[12] Schumpeter, *Theory of Economic Development*, p. 65.

[13] Schumpeter, *Theory of Economic Development*, p. 92.

[14] Schumpeter, *Theory of Economic Development*, p. 82 (note 2 from previous page).

[15] This terminology was introduced by Schumpeter at an early stage in his writing; see J. A. Schumpeter, *Das Wesen und der Hauptinhalt der theoretischen Nationalökonomie*, Munich and Leipzig: Duncker und Humblot, 1908; see especially pp. 86–7.

[16] Schumpeter, *Theory of Economic Development*, p. 81 (note 2); emphasis in original.

[17] Schumpeter, *Theory of Economic Development*, p. 93.

[18] Schumpeter, *Theory of Economic Development*, p. 93.

[19] Schumpeter, *Theory of Economic Development*, p. 93.

[20] This would align Schumpeter with other economists who propose a model under the heading of 'expressive rationality'. For one example of this, see S. H. Heap, 'Expressive Rationality: Is Self-worth Just Another Kind of Preference?', in U. Maki (ed.), *The Economic World View: Studies in the Ontology of Economics*, Cambridge: Cambridge University Press, 2001, pp. 98–113.

[21] Schumpeter, *Capitalism, Socialism and Democracy*, p. 132.

[22] This interpretation of Schumpeter, while not universal, is supported by Richard Arena and Paul-Marie Romani when they argue that while the entrepreneur can be considered to be an exogenous factor in Schumpeter's analysis, and thus a potential weakness in the structure of his work, this is not an accurate reading: 'If, instead, we consider entrepreneurship as the form of social leadership prevailing under capitalism, this critique loses its force. . . . Once these [capitalist] dynamics are analysed within a methodological framework that combines economic theory with sociology

and history . . . they clearly reflect an endogenous process of change' – R. Arena and P.-M. Romani, 'Schumpeter on Entrepreneurship', in R. Arena and C. Dangel-Hagnaner (eds), *The Contribution of Joseph Schumpeter to Economics: Economic Development and Institutional Change*, London: Routledge, 2002, pp. 167–83 (p. 181).

[23] See especially I. M. Kirzner, *Competition and Entrepreneurship*, Chicago, IL: University of Chicago Press, 1973.

[24] I. M. Kirzner, 'Uncertainty, Discovery, and Human Action: A Study of the Entrepreneurial Profile in the Misesian System', in I. M. Kirzner (ed.), *Method, Process, and Austrian Economics: Essays in Honor of Ludwig von Mises*, Lexington MA: Lexington Books, 1982, pp. 139–59 (p. 149).

[25] Kirzner, 'Uncertainty, Discovery, and Human Action', p. 150.

[26] Kirzner, 'Uncertainty, Discovery, and Human Action', p. 155.

[27] S. Johnson, *Where Good Ideas Come From: The Seven Patterns of Innovation*, London: Penguin, 2011.

[28] Johnson, *Where Good Ideas Come From*, pp. 84–7.

[29] R. Koppl, 'Entrepreneurial Behavior as a Human Universal', in M. Minniti (ed.), *Entrepreneurship: The Engine of Growth, Vol. 1 – People*, Westport, CT: Praeger, 2007, pp. 1–19 (pp. 1–2).

[30] This theme is prominent in Peter Sedgwick's theological consideration of enterprise; see P. Sedgwick, *The Enterprise Culture*, London: SPCK, 1992. Michael Volland bases his theological understanding of enterprise on his definition of an entrepreneur: 'A visionary who, in partnership with God and others, challenges the status quo by energetically creating and innovating in order to shape something of kingdom value' – M. Volland, *The Minister as Entrepreneur: Leading and Growing the Church in an Age of Rapid Change*, London: SPCK, 2015, p. 51.

[31] See the discussion in Volland's book, in which he explains the difference between greed and enterprise: Volland, *Minister as Entrepreneur*, pp. 19–24.

[32] For two examples of studies that in different ways corroborate these six aspects of entrepreneurial behaviour, see J. C. Collins and J. I. Porras, *Built to Last: Successful Habits of Visionary Companies*, New York: HarperCollins, 1994; and D. Priestly, *Entrepreneur Revolution: How to Develop Your Entrepreneurial Mindset and Start a Business that Works*, Chichester: Capstone, 2013. Another more anecdotal source is biographical and autobiographical material connected to successful entrepreneurs.

[33] This is corroborated by the other three uses of this word-group in Philippians. At 1.7 Paul describes the sharing or participation he has with his fellow Christians in the defence and confirmation of the gospel, and then at 4.14 and 4.15 he addresses the two separate themes of the Christians in Philippi participating in his distress, and then participating in the matter of giving and receiving.

[34] G. D. Fee, *Paul's Letter to the Philippians: The New International Commentary on the New Testament*, Grand Rapids, MI: Eerdmans, 1995, p. 82; emphasis in original. The only occurrence of the word in the Septuagint, the Greek translation of the Old Testament, is at Leviticus 6.2, where it describes a deposit or something at the disposal of various business partners. This is also reflected in the non-biblical usages of the word *koinonia*, which often means partnership in a business sense; see G. Kittel (ed.), trans. G. W. Bromiley, *Theological Dictionary of the New Testament, Volume 3*, Grand Rapids, MI: Eerdmans, 1965, p. 798, notes 5 and 6.

[35] The contrast between prophecy and fortune telling is set out clearly at Deuteronomy 18.9–22, where practices such as divination, augury, sorcery and the consulting of the dead are set in strong opposition to prophecy, which speaks only of the reality of God's purposes.

[36] W. Brueggemann, *Theology of the Old Testament: Testimony, Dispute, Advocacy*, Minneapolis, MN: Fortress Press, 1997, p. 626.

[37] J. Goldingay, *Old Testament Theology, Volume 1: Israel's Gospel*, Downers Grove, IL: InterVarsity Press, 2003, p. 678.

[38] W. Brueggemann, *The Prophetic Imagination*, 2nd edn, Minneapolis, MN: Fortress Press, 2001, p. 68.

[39] See in particular 1 Samuel 10.1–13; 19.18–24; 1 Kings 22.19–24; 2 Kings 2.9–15.

[40] See Acts 11.27–28; 13.1–3; 15.27–32; 21.10–11.

Chapter 4

Closing the gulf: a Christian voice for enterprise in the world

My argument has now developed through a number of stages. I have suggested that there is a real gulf between the market economy of this world and the kingdom of God. This is reflected particularly in the way that money is a rival to the promises of God, and in the way the scarcity underpinning market economics is set in contrast with the abundance of God's kingdom. I have expressed concerns over some attempts to bridge this gulf, and have argued that the theme of enterprise is particularly well placed to help in this regard. To this end I have examined at some length the important characteristics of enterprise when it is properly integrated into economic theory. I have also considered enterprise theologically and have suggested that a world view that takes God seriously resonates at a deep level with the way entrepreneurs experience the world. In feeling for a theology of enterprise I have tried to demonstrate that entrepreneurs, like prophets, instinctively revel in the abundance that is God's hallmark on earth, recognised in creation and above all else in the resurrection promise and the work of the Holy Spirit. In sum, I have concluded that enterprise shows us a particularly creative and powerful way in which human individuals and society can be shaped so as to allow God's purposes to flourish.

How then might these insights be applied? I wish to give a preliminary answer to this question by reflecting on some of my own experiences as an entrepreneur and a Christian, in action at different times both in the commercial marketplace and in the third sector. Beyond this I add some more conceptual thoughts about enterprise within the economy taken as a whole, and separately about the potential overlap between enterprise and church practice and ministry.

4.1 The Christian entrepreneur in action

It is tempting to try and build an intricate framework of advice or guidance for individual entrepreneurs, based on theological principles. However, enterprise is not at heart a formulaic thing. It is a lived thing, made real and given expression through actual experiences. I wish now therefore to reflect on four different life experiences of mine when I was engaged in entrepreneurial behaviour. My aim is to uncover how these experiences may have included a sense of the nearness of the kingdom of God. In sharing them my hope is that Christians who are setting up and running businesses might be affirmed, and that they too might learn to recognise the ways God's purposes are being played out through their activities.

> 'Enterprise shows us a particularly creative and powerful way in which human individuals and society can be shaped so as to allow God's purposes to flourish.'

In doing so I do not want to give the impression that a Christian entrepreneur will be more successful in business terms than any other entrepreneur. Nor do I want to give any space to the idea that God will somehow bless certain people with prosperity if they are obedient to God. Rather, my hope is that an entrepreneur who is informed by theology will be better equipped to understand the underlying value of what she or he does, and will be able to make connections between, on the one hand, the market economy in which enterprise plays its part and, on the other, the features of a world in which God is recognised and given honour and glory. It is in these connections that human faithfulness is discovered and God's purposes are revealed.

In 1988, at the age of 21, I established my own business. My aim was to enter the UK toy market with a new board game and alongside this to license a different game design to an existing manufacturer. The board game that I produced myself was called *Commotion*, aimed at the family market. With no prior experience to call upon I had to learn quickly as I oversaw the production aspect and the more important task of selling into the retailers. In the end *Commotion* was not a notable commercial success, although it was stocked by some national multiples and a good number of smaller toy shops.

Another game design of mine, *Speaker's Corner*, was offered to established manufacturers through an agent, but in the end was not taken up. It was a time when setbacks were mixed in with more positive moments and when persistence was needed above all else. Some of the decisions I made were poor, lacking in attentiveness to the real situations I faced.

At the time I did not make any particular theological connections to my activities as a very green entrepreneur, but as I look back I remember times of anxiety. I believe my tendency was to be too focused on attempting to forge my own success, rather than being in tune with what was happening around me. In short, I was not really operating properly as an entrepreneur, both because my motives were skewed and because my attentiveness was lacking. In market economy terms, I had fully understood neither the market I was trying to enter, nor the entrepreneurial energy I felt within myself. Interpreted theologically, the partnerships I was attempting to build were not rooted properly in a confidence in God's generosity towards others and me.

In 1991 I turned my own business into a part-time or hobby activity and became the production manager at Monkeypuzzle Ltd, a small giftware company based in Fakenham, Norfolk. While my primary role was to contribute to new product designs and oversee the production process, I also assisted the sales manager at trade fairs. Because the company was small, with some 20 people involved, including outworkers, there was a strong sense of working together and a shared excitement when a new product was launched or a significant order received. The trade fairs were exhausting, partly because the accommodation budget was minimal, but I recall still the energy that was released when the imaginations of our customers were caught by something we had offered them. We were displaying our product lines in competition with many other small businesses, but the sense of camaraderie was strong and we shared in others' triumphs even as we sought to outdo them ourselves.

As I reflect on these experiences I can appreciate the entrepreneurial characteristics of the owner and managing director. He had a particular skill for recognising what would make a good product, and the energy to follow up signs of success. In so doing he gave paid employment to a number of people, although the skills needed to manage them did not come so instinctively to him. He was ready to make personal sacrifices when times were hard, but my impression was that he found it difficult not to exercise control over the business in ways that were sometimes inappropriate or lacking in generosity. It was not always a happy place to work and people were not always nurtured creatively. A theological interpretation would suggest that some of the 'resurrection promise' ways of understanding the world were under-represented or absent. In particular, the apparent need to control did seem to have a dragging effect on the flourishing of the business and on the perceived value and contribution of the various stakeholders.

In purely market terms the business was struggling, with cash-flow problems, partly because the UK economy was in a downturn in the early 1990s, but also I believe because of some issues within the company. Interpreted theologically, there might have been a weakening of imaginative possibilities akin to the behaviour of Jesus' enemies, who failed to see or understand the generous resurrection world view he represented and described. The energy the business had contained in previous years had faded, in the same way that the national energy released by the spirit of prophecy had faded at different times in Israel, thus leading the nation to lose its true sense of vocation even while apparently being secure in its cautious approach.

By 1999 I was serving as an assistant curate at St Matthew's Church, Thorpe Hamlet, in the Diocese of Norwich. I put most of my entrepreneurial energies during that year into a project marking the millennium. The project involved making a video pageant called *The Old East Road*. While primarily a piece of social enterprise, it had commercial aspects, including the production of several thousand video cassettes for sale and a week of live drama shows. A large number of people came to be involved, and the nature of the project meant that it evolved and came to life as it unfolded. A particular feature was the inclusion on equal terms of a wide variety of people, who became co-creators of the final pageant, and the inclusion of local businesses both as financial sponsors and as participants. It was an organic and a broadly based piece of enterprise.

Although this project was a success, it could have failed in two main ways. First, the technical vision could have been impossible to carry through. In fact this nearly happened. An editing suite at the local university proved impossible to access successfully, but a small local media business run from someone's home came to the rescue. The business owner caught the vision of the project and in effect cross-subsidised most of the costs so as to bring it to fruition through his own goodwill and enthusiasm. Second, the project could have failed if the various community groups had not seen the community vision embraced by *The Old East Road*. This vision had to be worked for and constantly articulated; at times it was challenging work. However, at the heart of it lay the realisation that the pageant would not be complete if the different parts of the community were not all represented, and a sense that the actual road through the community was equally 'owned' by everyone.

Superficially the connection between the video pageant and the Christian faith was to do with the marking of the 2,000 years since the birth of Jesus Christ. In addition, much but not all of the driving energy came from church members. However, there was on reflection I believe a deeper connection between the project and Christianity because of its entrepreneurial nature. *The Old East Road* sat lightly to the inherited structures within the community and brought a fresh openness and equality to bear. Significant local institutions, such as the schools and the Sea Cadets, were placed on a level with other lower-profile groups and individuals. This was not an imposed thing, rather it emerged out of the entrepreneurial creativity of the whole project. Interpreted theologically, these features cohere with a resurrection world view, in which a radical equality is given by God in the abundance of his life-giving love.

In 2012 I was asked to develop on behalf of Chelmsford Diocese a resource to encourage Christian prayer and behaviour in everyday life. Many top-down examples of such things exist, but my instinctive aim was to find something that was attentive to people's own situations and that would also be a 'commercial' success. After considerable research I developed what came to be called the *Chelmsford Holding Cross*, made from old pews and laser-etched with the great commandment from the Bible. Eventually 15,000 were made and distributed, most of them sold at a cost-covering price.

Obviously, in this case the product was clearly Christian, but I was aware of deeper connections to God's purposes as expressed through entrepreneurial behaviour. My greater experience had led me to recognise better the moments when the hopes and imaginations of potential customers were engaged. While there were design features that contributed to the success of the *Chelmsford Holding Cross*, these were not merely clever inventions. Instead they arose out of and responded attentively to the aspirations of the potential purchasers. My theological interpretation is that what Paul described in his letters as the partnership, or enterprise, of the Holy Spirit had been richly embraced in this project.

What I have tried to demonstrate in this section is neither a precise formula for applying a theology of enterprise in practice nor a tight set of rules to follow, but that points of contact between theology and enterprise are there to be found in the real world, and not merely in theoretical terms. Such points of contact are living things and are to be discovered fresh in each unique situation, even while the overarching framework has an integrity of its own, given in God's revelation.

4.2 Enterprise as a God-given part of the economy

If it is true that enterprise is a powerful means whereby not just the individual activities of entrepreneurs but also the economy as a whole is brought into a closer alignment with God's purposes, it is something that should be encouraged by Christians in a general, macroeconomic way. This is not to provide carte blanche. Rather, it is to ensure that the theological insights offered earlier in my argument are considered and, where appropriate, taken up in the practical world of the economy. In general this will mean that an emphasis on central government economic planning would be unhelpful. This is because such planning will tend to try and second-guess the creative energies that enterprise brings to bear. In theological terms this will simply reinforce the gulf between faith and economics because the 'enterprise' found in the resurrection promise, in the work of the Holy Spirit and in prophecy will be pushed to one side and overlooked. However, I am not suggesting that there is no role for government. Rather, its role is of particular importance in fostering features of society that will encourage this theologically understood vision of enterprise.

One very important element within this 'framing' of society's expectations and assumptions is the need to disengage enterprise from the instrumental rationality that can all too easily dominate it. It is all too possible for enterprise to be understood in terms of personal greed. Instead it must be re-imagined as an energy that is aligned much more with the work of the Holy Spirit. Government has a battery of tools at its disposal, both in terms of regulation and education, which should be deployed to help in this exercise of re-imagination. For example, the connection between successful business enterprises and the provision of valued and vocational jobs should be reinforced. The rationality underlying entrepreneurial behaviour would therefore be aligned properly with the theological truths at the heart of the resurrection.

Government sets the framework within which businesses operate, notably, in the UK, as set out in the Companies Acts. In the early era of limited companies the Articles of Association was a significant document. It laid the foundation for what the company in question was intending to do and where it saw its 'home', both within the flow of time and with reference to place. In short, it anchored the company's expression of enterprise securely within the wider community, its history and its geography. Changes in corporate law now mean that the Articles of Association are completely generic and all-encompassing. Enterprise is no longer rooted in anything. Instead it is at the beck and call of the pursuit of so-called 'shareholder value', slave to an instrumental rationality that in fact threatens the very essence of enterprise and replaces it with management.

> **'It is all too possible for enterprise to be understood in terms of personal greed.'**

There are many examples of companies that have lost sight of their place in history and their geographical heritage. Company archivists have been made redundant and long-established geographical loyalties have been dissolved in the quest for marginal cost improvements. Of course, any company must be well run and profitable, but my argument is that for enterprise to flourish in its richest sense, any business must be truly rooted in the world. It might be too strong to require every company of a certain size and age to have a robust archivist function, but this is worthy of consideration. Similarly, ways could be explored of encouraging businesses to reinforce and enhance their connections with the places in which they operate. There are some good examples of this, although often such activities are understood as being about 'corporate responsibility', which in turn is justified for instrumental reasons linked to short-term competitive advantage.

> **'A company that took seriously its embedded place in the world would begin to rediscover some of the "family" aspects of successful enterprise.'**

A company that took seriously its embedded place in the world would begin to rediscover some of the 'family' aspects of successful enterprise. Any family has its 'archive' of photos and other memories, which root it in the flow of history. Families also have a sense of their geographical situation and loyalties. The same can be true for businesses, as Richard Turnbull has explained with reference to the great UK Quaker enterprises of the eighteenth and nineteenth centuries.[1] My argument has tried to show that when a company takes this 'family' aspect seriously, its efforts to be enterprising in the richest, theological sense will be enhanced because it will be properly attentive to the world in which it operates, not merely seeing it as an instrument for its own marginal gain. When a business does understand itself in this way, it becomes a valued and trusted partner in a community, cherished as part of the place in which it is located and as part of the developing story and history of that community, while all the time operating profitably and providing a return for the various factors of production.

Finally, this sense in which enterprise is properly embedded in a community is mirrored theologically on a bigger scale. The local community begins in turn to become properly embedded within a vision for the wider world that is aligned with God's purposes. The changes and developments in real communities reflect more closely the changes and developments that Christians look to as God's purposes are worked out. Put another way, the gulf between faith and economics has been made less daunting through a carefully understood application of enterprise. This is because the resurrection promise, the work of the Holy Spirit and the message of the prophets are all truly embedded in the life of the world and are not merely abstract ideas detached from time and place. Enterprise is a very practical way these theological truths are played out in the world.

4.3 THE CHRISTIAN ENTREPRENEUR AS A 'MINISTER' IN THE CHURCH

Michael Volland describes the Church as, broadly speaking, an organisation within which enterprise is not highly valued. He identifies concerns connected to materialism, greed, consumerism and personal gain, as well as a worry about a lack of collaboration and a tendency for exclusion.[2] However, Volland's argument is that such descriptions are a distortion of what enterprise truly should be. His research among church ministers in the Durham Diocese of the Church of England reveals that there is plenty of local enterprise happening in the life of the Church, and that this has a powerful and positive impact. Volland's own conclusion consists of 11 suggestions for the Church.[3] The first of these asks for a more positive language around enterprise in general within the Church, which leads into subsequent suggestions about encouraging more candidates for ministry with entrepreneurial flair, and then the encouraging of these entrepreneurs in their ongoing ministries at local, regional and national levels.

Volland's approach is largely practical. He is concerned to describe enterprise as a useful tool that can be put to work in the service of building up the Church. He does give a theological account of enterprise,[4] but this culminates in an examination of entrepreneurial people in Scripture and in the life of the Church. However, if my own argument about the theology of enterprise is brought to bear, and if it is therefore the case that enterprise is an aspect of human action that brings the world closer to God, it is easy to sustain the view that enterprise should be encouraged in the life of the Church, but with a slightly different emphasis. Volland's suggestion in effect sees enterprise as a secular tool to be taken up by the Church as a useful instrument for its growth. I would rather understand enterprise in the life of the Church as part of a process of alignment whereby the world is aligned better with God's kingdom. Another way of understanding this is by seeing enterprise in the life of the Church as an element within the apostolic call placed on Christians, rather than as a means for encouraging *discipleship*.

Christians are to be both disciples and apostles. A disciple is a follower who walks in the steps of another. A Christian disciple walks in the way of Jesus Christ. An apostle is someone who is sent out, bearing a message. A Christian apostle is sent out to take the message of the good news in Christ Jesus, that the kingdom of God has drawn near. Enterprise is not at heart a 'disciple' concept. Entrepreneurs do not follow. Instead they are attentive to what is happening and they pioneer new ways, bringing a fresh product or service into a market or even creating a new market out of people's hopes and desires. Entrepreneurs are therefore much more akin to apostles. The theology of enterprise that I articulated earlier found points of contact between the enterprise of economic theory and the good news of the reality of God's kingdom. My claim now is that if the Church really is to take enterprise seriously, it must not be treated as a tool for discipleship but as an expression of apostleship.

The New Testament contains accounts of both discipleship and apostleship but I would like to argue that the trajectory is towards apostleship. Jesus only calls disciples to follow him so that he can send them out with the good news. The 'following' is a step on the way to 'being sent'. The task the Church faces is not to grow itself into a bigger organisation for its own sake. Instead its task is to send out entrepreneurs – in the theologically informed sense – to align the world more closely to the kingdom of God. This means, of course, that the Church needs to be strong and thriving so that this 'sending' can happen regularly and with energy.

One practical suggestion that therefore arises is that churches should place more emphasis on 'sending well' rather than solely on welcoming. The welcoming task can all too easily become analogous to the marketing task in the secular world. In my experience, a church that is good at welcoming is first of all good at sending. This makes perfect sense because people will be welcomed not with a view to getting something from them, be it money or time or talents, but to equipping them to go on their way with the good news. Such a welcome is far more life-giving and attuned to God's purposes.

Furthermore, I would like to suggest that the language and practice of enterprise in the life of the Church is specifically associated with this call to be apostolic as Christians. If the Church is to place more emphasis on 'sending well', it will need to embrace the language and attributes of enterprise far more emphatically. Christians need to be encouraged to be a lot more attentive to the presence of God within the ordinary things of life, including the ubiquitous buying and selling that happens in the marketplace. They also need to be far more aware of the way God is shaping the flow of 'ordinary' history in 'ordinary' places. The true task of enterprise in the eyes of a Christian is to be found in the heart of the ordinary business of life, part of the overarching movement of aligning the world to God's kingdom. Of course, enterprise can sometimes be subverted and stripped of its true purpose, even at the hands of Christians. If, however, it is clearly named as an apostolic expression, I believe enterprise will help bring about a renewing of hope and joyfulness within the churches.

4.4 A PERSONAL ENDNOTE

My own experience of life in general, and Christian ministry in particular, has led me to affirm the place for enterprise because when I have been entrepreneurial I have found people's imaginations caught and new possibilities made real in a very tangible way. Enterprise is not rooted in theories or even vision statements. It is based on attentiveness and the ability to adapt, while remaining true to core motivations and to a particular vision of the world. Enterprise does bring new things about, but not principally out of inventiveness, rather out of the latent hopes and aspirations of a community and the very nature of creation as sustained by God.

On one level, Christian entrepreneurs are no different from any other entrepreneurs. However, I believe enterprise can be put at the service of the gospel, as well as in the life of the Church, which often seems to struggle with an entrepreneurial approach. This is perhaps because of its calling to guard the truths and promises of God, much as when Paul wrote to Timothy: 'guard what has been entrusted to you' (1 Timothy 6.20a). Entrepreneurs do not necessarily make instinctively good guardians, being less defensively minded. Enterprise can be a risky business and it is sometimes hard to evaluate an entrepreneur's progress in a scientific manner. But the same is true of prophets, of the powerful influence of the Holy Spirit and of the way God's resurrection promise shapes the world in which we live. At a recent gathering of ordained ministers in secular employment, which I had been asked to lead, I spoke about enterprise. The reaction was mixed but it was very striking when we ended with 'the grace' and when some of those present voiced the interpretation I had talked about: 'The grace of our Lord Jesus Christ, and the love of God, and the *enterprise* of the Holy Spirit, be with us all, evermore; Amen.' At a stroke it changed the feel of our concluding prayer, sending us on our way rather than binding us back together.

My own practical experience of attempting to be entrepreneurial, alongside the day-to-day way I try to live out my Christian faith apostolically, makes me feel instinctively that the two must be connected. The arguments and suggestions in this publication set out some reasons why this might be so. My hope is that they will be a particular encouragement to Christians who are engaged in enterprise of all varieties, both in the world of business and in the life of the Church, that the purposes of God might thereby be advanced.

4.5 SUMMARY

Starting from my claim that enterprise shows us a particularly creative and powerful way human individuals and society can be shaped so as to allow God's purposes to flourish and the gulf between faith and economics to be bridged, I go on to describe from my own experience what such points of contact might be like in practice. This is not part of a detailed formula by which a theology of enterprise can be used to create a successful business. Instead I argue that an entrepreneur who is informed by theology will be better equipped to understand the underlying value of his or her activities and better able to make connections between God's purposes and human endeavours. I then suggest that in a macroeconomic sense, particular attention should be paid to the anchoring of enterprise in the history and geography of communities and the fostering of the 'family' aspects of business, whatever size the company in question. This reflects the way the theology of enterprise is rooted in the flow of time and the reality of particular places. A positive example of this would be the Quaker businesses of the eighteenth and nineteenth centuries. I suggest that enterprise is thereby potentially a very practical way by which economics and faith are brought into closer alignment. Finally, I look to possible applications in the life of the Church. I argue that it is a mistake to see enterprise as merely a tool for the building up of the Church. Rather, I suggest that enterprise is an expression of the apostolic mission of the Church, to send believers out with the good news of the nearness of God's kingdom. I argue that, paradoxically, a sending Church will be far better at welcoming and far better integrated with the wider world. I also argue that the language and practices of entrepreneurial behaviour are closely connected to the apostolic call and that these should therefore deliberately be encouraged and supported in church life and ministry.

> **'An entrepreneur who is informed by theology will be better equipped to understand the underlying value of his or her activities.'**

Notes to Chapter 4

[1] R. Turnbull, *Quaker Capitalism: Lessons for Today*, Oxford: CEME, 2014.
[2] M. Volland, *The Minister as Entrepreneur: Leading and Growing*, London: SPCK, 2015, pp. 15–19.
[3] Volland, *Minister as Entrepreneur*, pp. 122–3.
[4] Volland, *Minister as Entrepreneur*, pp. 47–65.